HOW DOES AN OCTOPUS SLEEP?

Discover the ways your favorite animals sleep and what makes them special

OCTAVIO PINTOS · MARTÍN IANNUZZI

ORANGE
M·O·S·Q·U·I·T·O

EXPLORE AND DESCRIBE

↓

Sleep is as important as eating, self-defense, and reproduction. It is one of life's principal biological mechanisms.

↓

Most animals have a daily pattern of activity and rest. All species need to sleep, from one-cell mechanisms to the most evolved. It is a way of relaxing the brain, slowing the metabolism, and reducing the need for food. Some species are more active during the day, some during the night, others sleep only partially or in short periods of rest.

In the pages of this book, you will discover a varied selection of animals who live in different regions and landscapes around the globe. Our world has such an infinity of species, either discovered or to be discovered, that it would be impossible to include all of them in a single book.

↓

CONTENTS

↓

Published in 2022 by Orange Mosquito

An Imprint of Welbeck Children's Limited

part of Welbeck Publishing Group.

Based in London and Sydney.

www.welbeckpublishing.com

Design and layout © Mosquito Books Barcelona, SL 2021
Text © Octavio Pintos and Martín Iannuzzi 2021
Illustration © Octavio Pintos and Martín Iannuzzi 2021
Translated by Howard Curtis
Publisher: Margaux Durigon
Production: Jess Brisley

ISBN: 9781914519260
eISBN: 9781914519277

Printed in China

10 9 8 7 6 5 4 3 2 1

FSC
www.fsc.org
MIX
Paper from
responsible sources
FSC® C020056

DEDICATED TO THOSE WHO ARE IN CONSTANT
SEARCH OF NEW AND UNKNOWN THINGS.

No animals were harmed in the making of this book, but a few were bribed into helping out.

HOW TO READ THIS BOOK

ANTHROPOMETRIC COMPARISON

Comparison of size between a person of 1.780 metres and the species.

LIFE EXPECTANCY

Length of time the species lives.

REPRODUCTION

How the species reproduces and gives birth.

HABITAT

Discover the place where each species lives.

GEOGRAPHICAL DISTRIBUTION

These coloured areas on the map show where the species lives and interacts with the ecosystem.

TIME OF SLEEP

Time when it rests: night, day or both.

IMPORTANT FACTS

These texts present extra facts about each species.

HOW IT SLEEPS

These coloured areas show the way each species rests.

HOURS OF SLEEP

Length of time it rests for.

ICONOGRAPHY

TAXONOMY (biological classification of life, scientists categorise living things according to their differences and similarities)

Phylum

Category of living creatures that share common features; e.g. vertebrates which are animals with a backbone.

Class

Phyla (plural for phylum) are divided into classes according to their most common characteristics; e.g. mammals are a class of vertebrates.

Order

Based on common characteristics, but more specific ones than in class; e.g. carnivores - meat-eating mammals.

LIFE ENVIRONMENT

Indicates animals that move by flying.

Air

Indicates animals that live In the ocean, sea, rivers or lakes.

Water

Indicates animals that move on land.

Land

Indicates animals that move on land and water.

Land and water

CONSERVATION STATUS

Out of danger

This conservation category of species is considered in no danger of disappearing.

Vulnerable

Refers to the conservation category of species with a high risk of extinction.

Endangered

Refers to the conservation category of species at greatest risk of extinction.

DIETARY TYPE

Depending on what the animals or insects eat, they are classified as herbivores, carnivores or omnivores.

Carnivores (meat eaters) **Herbivores** (plant eaters) **Omnivores** (eat both!)

SCIENTIFIC NAME

Name given to every organism — living or extinct. It is a two-part name, indicating genus (animals that are closely related; e.g. a horse and donkey) and species (e.g. all horses).

It searches for a place to sleep, narrows its eyes and remains still for long periods of time. Every now and again, for about 15 minutes, it rapidly changes color and contracts its tentacles.

It has brain waves associated with REM (rapid eye movement – a light sleep stage) sleep. This indicates that octopuses go through sleep cycles, just like humans and other vertebrates.

IT HAS A DEEP SLEEP SIMILAR TO HUMANS.

It experiences a ricochet effect: if it wakes up and can't get back to sleep, it has to catch up the next day.

Octopuses sleep at the bottom of the sea, searching out the quiet and darkness of marine crevasses.

While sleeping, an octopus makes rapid eye movements accompanied by convulsions. Its tentacles and body change color, blending into the surroundings.

It uses its siphon for breathing, the elimination of waste and squirting ink.

EYES
They can see polarised light.

→ **SIPHON**

It can adapt itself to go unobserved by predators, changing shape, color and skin texture.

The mouth, situated under the arms, has a hard, sharp chitinous beak – similar to that of a parrot.

THE ARMS REACH A LENGTH OF 14 FEET (4 M).

33 POUNDS (15 KG)

Adult octopuses can weigh up to 33 pounds (15 kg).

APPENDAGES

Its 2 rear appendages are used for walking on the sea bed while the others are used to search for food.

It has a complex nervous system and excellent eyesight. It is amongst the most intelligent vertebrates.

OCTOPUS

It is bilaterally symmetrical, with its mouth and beak situated in the center of its 8 limbs.

There are about 300 known species of octopus.

A deep sleeper

REPRODUCTION

During reproduction, the male uses a specially adapted arm to deposit a packet of sperm in the female's mantle cavity, after which he quickly ages and dies. The female lays the fertilized eggs in a lair and looks after them until the young are born, after which she also dies.

Taxonomy

Phylum: **invertebrate**
Class: **cephalopoda**
Order: **octopoda**

LIFE EXPECTANCY

UP TO 5 YEARS

Most species grow quickly, mature early and have a short life.

Octopuses have brains, however most of their nervous system is located in their tentacles, which are able to make decisions independently.

SUCKERS

They have an excellent sense of touch. Octopus suckers are equipped with chemoreceptors that allow them to sense the taste of what it touches. The arms cannot get tangled up because the sensors recognize the octopus's own skin or that of others.

GEOGRAPHICAL DISTRIBUTION

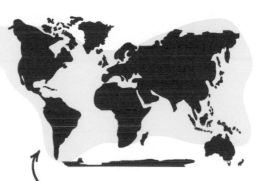

Found in all the oceans of the world, they are more common in warm waters and less common in cold waters.

HOW THEY MOVE

They move by taking in water and expelling it in order to propel themselves. When they feel threatened, they shoot out clouds of ink to confuse predators; they also do this when they are dreaming.

They have soft bodies that can change shape quickly, allowing them to get through small cracks.

MARINE HABITAT

They live in various regions of the ocean, such as coral reefs, deep waters and the sea bed.

They feed mainly on crustaceans, bristle worms, molluscs, clams, prawns, fish and other cephalopods.

Scientific name: **Octopus Vulgaris**

Dietary type: **carnivore**

Life environment: **water**

Conservation status: **out of danger**

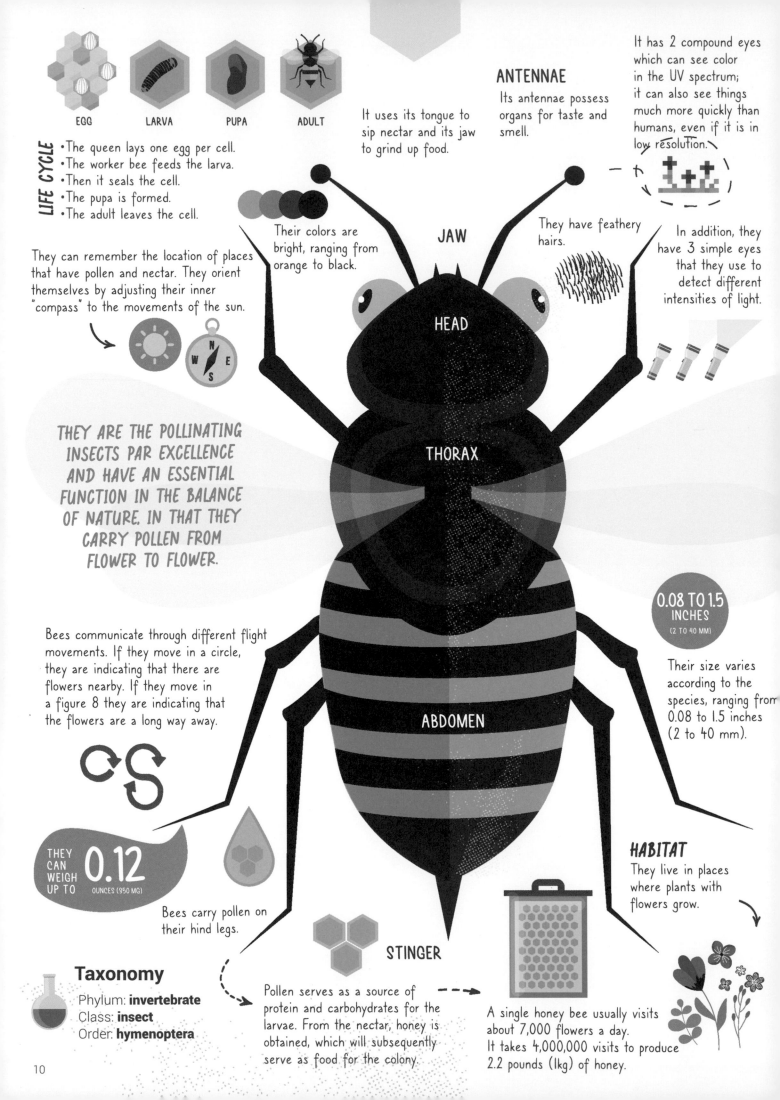

LIFE CYCLE

EGG   LARVA   PUPA   ADULT

- The queen lays one egg per cell.
- The worker bee feeds the larva.
- Then it seals the cell.
- The pupa is formed.
- The adult leaves the cell.

It uses its tongue to sip nectar and its jaw to grind up food.

ANTENNAE
Its antennae possess organs for taste and smell.

It has 2 compound eyes which can see color in the UV spectrum; it can also see things much more quickly than humans, even if it is in low resolution.

They have feathery hairs.

In addition, they have 3 simple eyes that they use to detect different intensities of light.

They can remember the location of places that have pollen and nectar. They orient themselves by adjusting their inner "compass" to the movements of the sun.

Their colors are bright, ranging from orange to black.

JAW

HEAD

THEY ARE THE POLLINATING INSECTS PAR EXCELLENCE AND HAVE AN ESSENTIAL FUNCTION IN THE BALANCE OF NATURE, IN THAT THEY CARRY POLLEN FROM FLOWER TO FLOWER.

THORAX

0.08 TO 1.5 INCHES (2 TO 40 MM)

Their size varies according to the species, ranging from 0.08 to 1.5 inches (2 to 40 mm).

Bees communicate through different flight movements. If they move in a circle, they are indicating that there are flowers nearby. If they move in a figure 8 they are indicating that the flowers are a long way away.

ABDOMEN

THEY CAN WEIGH UP TO **0.12** OUNCES (950 MG)

Bees carry pollen on their hind legs.

STINGER

HABITAT
They live in places where plants with flowers grow.

Taxonomy
Phylum: **invertebrate**
Class: **insect**
Order: **hymenoptera**

Pollen serves as a source of protein and carbohydrates for the larvae. From the nectar, honey is obtained, which will subsequently serve as food for the colony.

A single honey bee usually visits about 7,000 flowers a day. It takes 4,000,000 visits to produce 2.2 pounds (1kg) of honey.

BEE

SLEEPS IN THE HIVE

There are known to be more than 20,000 distinct subspecies divided into 7 families.

They do not have eyelids. When they sleep they → stop moving their antennae and reduce their metabolism to save energy.

They need to rest in order to have the energy to communicate → effectively with other bees.

A bee that has slept badly can cause disaster to the social life of the hive.

→ They sleep outside the cell but inside the hive, in the highest and quietest parts. Those who find themselves outside in bad weather can sleep amidst the flowers, attached to a stem or a branch.

Honey bees take turns sleeping in the hive. They only sleep by day if they do not have to collect nectar.

Hours of sleep: 30 / 90 minutes
Time of sleep: night.

GEOGRAPHICAL DISTRIBUTION

Found in all the continents of the world except Antarctica.

REPRODUCTION

The queen bee is the only one who can reproduce. She feeds on honey provided by the worker bees.

↓

LAYS 3,000 EGGS A DAY

Fertilized eggs will hatch as worker bees and unfertilized eggs as drones.

↓

The queens come from fertilized eggs containing royal jelly. The first queen bee that is born expels the current queen bee, since there can only be one per hive. The expelled queen bee will form a new hive with the workers who remain faithful to her.

20.000–60.000 BEES

THEY LIVE IN HIVES IN WHICH THERE ARE HIERARCHIES.

Queen

Emits pheromones and a buzz to attract drones, who make a nuptial journey to mate with her. She can store up to 5 million spermatozoa inside her, with which the eggs are fertilized.

Worker
Emits pheromones and a This bee's job is to make wax, to maintain the temperature of the hive, and to feed and defend the queen and the larvae.

Drone

These bees are male and lead an idle life until the queen mates with them; after which she kills them.

 LIFE EXPECTANCY

UP TO 4 YEARS

Workers live from 40 to 60 days. Drones live about 40 days. Queens may live up to 3 or 4 years.

 Royal jelly is a substance secreted by the hypopharyngeal glands in the heads of young worker bees.

Scientific name: **Anthophila**

 Dietary type: **herbivore**

 Life environment: **air**

 Conservation status: **vulnerable**

ANT
STAGGERS ITS SLEEP

IT IS ESTIMATED THAT THERE ARE BETWEEN 1,000 BILLION AND 10,000 BILLION ANTS LIVING ON EARTH.

Ants sleep in shifts, so there is always someone working. Workers, collectors and soldiers share a partial sleep.

250 NAPS

They take 250 naps a day that can last up to one minute. In total, about 4 or 5 hours a day.

Hours of sleep: 4/5 hours.
Time of sleep: night and day.

The queen ant can take naps of up to 9 minutes but only does so inside the nest.

DEEP SLEEP PHASE

Ants can go into a deep sleep. During this phase, their jaw and the antennae movements are reduced by about 65%, although they can move involuntarily.

Ants can sleep at any time. Living below ground, they have no notion of day or night..

When they sleep, their fellow workers may bump into them. This does not interrupt the ant's sleep or irritate them, they just snooze on and only wake up to continue with their work in the nest.

GEOGRAPHICAL DISTRIBUTION

Found all over the world, except in Arctic and Antarctic regions and a few inhospitable islands.

Worker ants look after the eggs and larvae, in addition to providing food for the queen. They take care of all tasks relating to the construction and maintenance of the nest. They look for food, feed the male bees, and even wage war.

WORKER ANT

MALE   FEMALE

The queen ant lays **1,200 eggs a day.**

REPRODUCTION

When larvae or pupae are born, they are gathered in groups of the same size and same age to make sure that each one receives sufficient food and attention.

LIFE CYCLE

Male ants and young females have wings. One day they take flight and mate. The males immediately die and the females look for a new home. There, after laying eggs and losing their wings forever, they begin a new colony and restart the cycle.

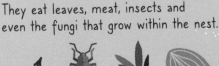

They eat leaves, meat, insects and even the fungi that grow within the nest.

Scientific name: *Formicidae*

Dietary type: **omnivore**

Life environment: **land**

Conservation status: **out of danger**

They have 2 strong jaws, which they use to carry food, manipulate objects, build nests and defend themselves.

With their jaws they can lift up to

100
TIMES THEIR OWN WEIGHT.

ANTENNAE

The antennae of the head are extremely important, they are used to sense currents of air and detect textures.

THEY CAN BE HERBIVORES OR CARNIVORES DEPENDING ON THE SPECIES.

← EYES

With their eyes they sense movements around them, although it is hard for them to distinguish shapes and objects, since their eyesight is weak.

HEAD

Taxonomy
Phylum: **invertebrate**
Class: **insect**
Order: **hymenoptera**

They vary between 0.08 and 1 inch. In east and central Africa there is a species of giant ant that measures 2 inches (5 cm).

0.08 TO 1 INCH (2 TO 25MM)

HABITAT
They live below the ground, in dark, hidden places and in green areas where there is a source of food.

THORAX
They have sectional bodies that include a prominent thorax, antennae, and legs.

SIX LEGS
They have six legs, joined to the thorax, with a claw situated at the end of each leg that helps them to climb and fasten onto different kinds of surfaces.

ABDOMEN
Most are red, black or yellow. Green is less common, and some tropical species have a metallic color.

LEGS

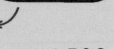

LIFE EXPECTANCY
A queen ant may live between 15 and 30 years, while workers only reach 3.

3 YEARS

THE COLONY
Usually situated in small natural cavities; they can occupy large spaces below the surface.

THEY ARE SOCIABLE
Ants live in an organized way, with each member performing a specific function.

The colony consists of a number of queen ants, thousands of worker ants and a few winged males.

13

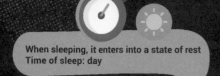

When sleeping, it enters into a state of rest
Time of sleep: day

Many sharks enters into a state of rest, as if asleep, while still moving. It can never entirely stop swimming, as it has no air bladder allowing it to float to the surface for oxygen.

To rest, it alternates periods of activity and inactivity, in which only one part of the brain sleeps – although it always has both eyes open.

Some species have structures called spiracles that allow them to breathe while resting at the bottom of the ocean.

A spiracle is a small opening behind each eye. This structure forces water through the gills so that these kinds of shark can be virtually still when resting.

AMPULLAE OF LORENZINI

System of pores in its head and snout, which allows it to detect electrical signals emitted by other animals.

WHILE THEY SWIM, THEY EXPERIENCE CYCLES OF CONSCIOUS AND LESS CONSCIOUS STATES.

DORSAL FIN

GILLS

Water, filled with oxygen, passes through the shark's gills and enters the blood stream. If a shark stops swimming, it suffocates and dies.

A shark leaves its mouth open as it advances through the ocean, a method it uses to breathe.

THEY CAN LOSE UP TO 1,000 TEETH A YEAR.

A shark's tooth takes about one week to fall out, and the new tooth can appear in a day.

Its skeleton is made up of cartilage, which allows it to swim with ease, flexibility and speed.

PECTORAL FIN

It does not close its eyes, because it does not have eyelids. In their place, it has a membrane called a nictitating membrane, which is translucent and covers the eyeball.

328 FEET (100 M)

Sharks can smell a single drop of blood from at least 328 feet (100 m) away. They use smell and sight to find possible victims, using surprise as a means of attack.

UP TO
60
FEET (18 M)

Its size varies according to the species. They range from 6.5 feet (2 m) to 60 feet (18 m), as in the case of the whale shark.

Sharks have been in existence for more than 400 million years.

400
MILLION
YEARS

SHARK

SLEEPS WHILE SWIMMING

There are more than 375 species of shark in the oceans of the world.

REPRODUCTION

Viviparous
The embryo develops in the mother's belly, in a special structure that allows it to receive the food and oxygen necessary to grow until the moment of birth.

Oviparous
The mother lays its eggs in the water, where the embryonic development is completed.

Ovoviviparous
The embryo is formed in an egg that hatches inside the mother's belly, where it develops before coming out.

Taxonomy
Phylum: **vertebrate**
Class: **fish**
Order: **lamniformes**

They give birth to one or two pups.

Its skin is rough and has tiny scales of the same material as its teeth, forming a resistant barrier that protects it.

CAUDAL FIN

ANAL FIN

/ The upper part of its body is dark in color and its lower parts either light or white. \

These species do not require large quantities of food to compensate for the energy spent on the long journeys they undertake.

HABITAT
They live in all the oceans of the world: warm, temperate and cold. In deep waters, open oceans and coasts..

LIFE EXPECTANCY

UP TO 30 YEARS

In their natural state they can live between 20 and 30 years.

GEOGRAPHICAL DISTRIBUTION

Sharks are found in all the oceans of the world. Some species migrate in search of food and water, of the right depth and temperature. They prefer tropical and temperate zones.

They feed on fish, crustaceans, molluscs, plankton, marine mammals and even other sharks.

Scientific name: *Selachimorpha*

Dietary type: **carnivore**

Life environment: **water**

Conservation status: **vulnerable**

Taxonomy

Phylum: **vertebrate**
Class: **fish**
Order: **syngnathiformes**

It has the ability to blend into its surroundings by changing its skin color or developing long filaments that make it look like a subaquatic plant.

HABITAT

It lives in different types of warm-water seas and oceans, where there are corals, algae and mangroves.

REPRODUCTION

Most species form monogamous partnerships, with male and female helping each other.

IT IS THE MALE THAT GETS PREGNANT.

The courtship process is very slow. It begins with the male turning around the female and producing clicking sounds.

For days, the couple remain together. During this time, they do a synchronized dance and the male demonstrates to the female that he is not incubating any other eggs. When the little ovocytes are ready, the couple grab each other by the tail and the female inserts them into the male.

EVERY SEAHORSE IS UNIQUE THEY ARE ALL BORN WITH PRO-TUBERANCES ON THE HEAD CALLED CROWNS. EACH ONE IS DIFFERENT AND MAKES IT POSSIBLE TO IDENTIFY INDIVIDUALS; SIMILAR TO FINGERPRINTS IN HUMANS.

LIFE EXPECTANCY

UP TO **5** YEARS

Its life expectancy varies between 1 and 5 years.

The male develops the embryos for 6 to 10 weeks, at the end of which time the fry are born.

6 TO 10 WEEKS

GEOGRAPHICAL DISTRIBUTION

Found in the tropical, subtropical and temperate oceans, the Atlantic, the Indian and the Pacific.

IT CAN GIVE BIRTH TO UP TO 400 FRY.

During the first days, the newborn enter and leave the father's ventral sac several times, as long as there is no danger outside.

As they grow, the fry can eat up to 3,000 times a day. When they become adults this is reduced to 50.

There are 54 species around the world

SEAHORSE
SLEEPS CLINGING TO A PLANT

Its eyes move independently of each other, helping them to spot and capture its prey.

PECTORAL FIN

WHEN SLEEPING. IT FALLS INTO A STATE OF REST

It usually rests at night, with its eyes open because it has no eyelids.

Hours of sleep: remains in a state of rest.
Time of sleep: night.

It has no teeth, but uses its snout to eat its prey whole.

To sleep, it wraps its tail around an aquatic plant so that the currents do not sweep it away.

Its tail curls with great strength and pressure. Sometimes it clings to other sea-horses to sleep.

It has no scales, but a frame made of bony plates.

DORSAL FIN

Its colors vary depending on the species, ranging between beige, black, grey, purple, orange and yellow.

Having both dorsal and pectoral fins, its movements are very slow.

Since it has no stomach, the process of digestion is very rapid, which forces it to eat constantly.

NOT A GOOD SWIMMER

It uses its dorsal fin to propel itself in the currents; but if it gets caught in turbulent waters, it may drown.

UP TO **14** INCHES (35 CM)

Its size varies depending on the species. The smallest can measure 5/8 inch (1.5 cm) and the largest reach 14 inches (35 cm).

It feeds on small crustaceans, fish larvae and plankton.

Scientific name: *Hippocampus*

Dietary type: **carnivore**

Life environment: **water**

Conservation status: **vulnerable**

Hours of sleep: 6 hours
Time of sleep: day

During the day it sleeps motionless in caves, under trunks and leaves; although it remains alert during its period of rest.
At night, it is active.

It comes out at the beginning of the evening to make its call and then spends the night hunting.

Tree frogs seek out cool, dark and damp places to sleep in.

It is believed that its eyes are adapted to its nocturnal lifestyle.

It has translucent eyelids with beautiful patterns that it uses for camouflage to hide from predators while it rests.

Most have gold-colored eyes and horizontal irises, typical of the genus *Litoria*.

Its tongue is sticky so that prey gets stuck on it; a technique it uses to catch small insects. With larger prey, the frog leaps on to its victim and forces it into its mouth, using its hands.

Its color depends on the temperature and color of its surroundings, ranging from brown to green.

LEGS

Its skin is thin and covered in mucus, which keeps it damp and sticky.

In winter, green tree frogs are hard to find as they hibernate.

Although frogs have lungs, they also absorb oxygen through the skin. Their damp skin encourages pathogenic agents which cause infections. For this reason, frogs also secrete peptides that destroy these pathogenic agents.

TREE
FROG

SLEEPS SHOWING ITS REMARKABLE EYELIDS.

It moves easily through vegetation to hunt the insects that are its food.

It can climb, thanks to the suckers it has on the palms of its hands.

It has large discs at the end of each leg, about 0.2 inches (5 mm) in diameter. These discs allow it to cling to surfaces as it climbs.

The green tree frog is a large species, in comparison with most other Australian species of frogs.

SUCKERS

The toes are joined together by a cutaneous membrane.

GEOGRAPHICAL DISTRIBUTION

Found in Australia, the south of North America, Central America and New Zealand.

HABITAT

Urban gardens, prairies and subtropical forests.

They are docile and have adapted to life close to human habitation.

LIFE EXPECTANCY

The species has an average life expectancy of 16 years in captivity. In the wild, it is lower, due to predation.

16 YEARS

UP TO 4 INCHES (10 CM)

It can grow up to 10 centimetres/ 4 inches in length.

The secretions of the frog's skin have antiviral and antiseptic properties that can prove useful in pharmaceutical products.

REPRODUCTION

| The female lays **200-300 eggs** | The process is repeated for **2 days** | Result: **3,000 eggs** | Incubation period **3 days** | The water must be between **28° 38°** | |

Metamorphosis (from tadpole to frog) takes between 2 and 3 months, and sexual maturity almost 2 years.

Its diet consists mainly of insects and spiders.

Scientific name: *Litoria Caerulea*

Dietary type: **carnivore**

Life environment: **land, water**

Conservation status: **vulnerable**

BUTTERFLY
Gather together to sleep

There are more than 165,000 species, classified into 127 families.

Its whole body is covered in small sensitive hairs and its membranous wings are covered in scales.

The scales alter the direction of the light, producing bright, shiny, iridescent colors.

Its tongue is the shape of a long snout. It curls like a spiral when it is at rest and straightens completely in order to suck nectar from the flowers that it pollinates.

REPRODUCTION

Male and female butterflies find each other through the movements of their wings and using smell. Courtship is based on particular flight maneuvers when the males cover the females with their pheromones.

To lay their hundreds of eggs, females look for places with abundant plants.

LIFE CYCLE

From the egg emerges a caterpillar that will be transformed into a pupa and then it grows into an adult. In the pupa state, it does not eat and undergoes a combination of changes known as metamorphosis.

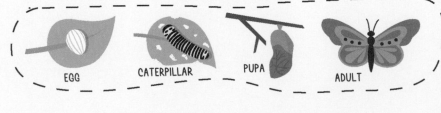

EGG   CATERPILLAR   PUPA   ADULT

Caterpillars feed on leaves and adults absorb nectar and other liquid substances.

THORAX (BEHIND ITS HEAD)

The flight muscles that control the wings and legs are concentrated here.

ABDOMEN (BACK OF ITS BODY)

The abdomen houses the butterfly's digestive, excretory, and reproductive systems.

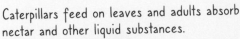

Scientific name: *Lepidoptera*

Dietary type: **herbivore**

Life environment: **air**

Conservation status: **out of danger**

Nocturnal: they wake at dusk, their bodies are usually voluminous and their wings very heavy; they are always open even in rest.

Diurnal: they tend to have thinner, lighter bodies. When they are at rest their wings are vertically folded.

Butterflies sleep beneath leaves which serve as camouflage – to protect themselves from birds that get up early in search of food.

BRIGHTLY COLORED BUTTERFLIES REST MORE EXPOSED AND WITH THEIR WINGS UNFOLDED. WARNING BIRDS THAT THEY MAY BE POISONOUS.

They almost always sleep hanging upside down, clinging to a leaf like this requires minimal energy.

Hours of sleep: 6 hours
Time of sleep: night and day

They sleep in groups to protect themselves from predators.

WINGS

These regulate their body temperature and are involved in the process of courtship.

0.2 INCH (3 MM) → **12** INCHES (30 CM)

Their size varies between 0.2 inch and 12 inches. The largest is the Queen Alexandra's Birdwing, which lives in Papua New Guinea.

HABITAT

Open gardens, subtropical meadows and forests

GEOGRAPHICAL DISTRIBUTION

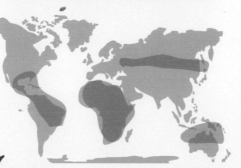

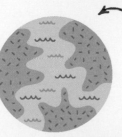

More than 200 species migrate to other regions due to climatic conditions or to search for new vegetation to host their larvae.

LIFE EXPECTANCY

UP TO **9** MONTHS

The smallest usually live approximately one week, while some species have an average life expectancy of about 9 months.

Taxonomy

Phylum: **invertebrate**
Class: **insect**
Order: **lepidoptera**

Found in hot tropical regions of Africa, Asia, America and Australia.

BEAK

The beak is strong and curves downward with a lower jaw that is larger than the upper; it can be different colors, such as yellow, orange, or pink, with a black tip.

Their beaks are lined with rows of plates that filter the food and the salt out of the water they ingest.

A healthy, well-fed flamingo is very bright in color.

It can submerge its head underwater and hold its breath for long periods in search of food.

THEY CAN FLY HUNDREDS OF MILES TO FEED THEMSELVES AND THEN RETURN TO THE COLONY.

It reaches flight speeds of 30 to 37 miles (50 to 60 km) per hour. Flamingos that fly in groups usually form V shapes to conserve energy against the wind.

Their plumage is of different pink or fuchsia shades.

LIFE EXPECTANCY

UP TO 40 YEARS

Their life expectancy varies between 25 and 40 years.

UP TO 9 POUNDS (4 KG).

UP TO 5 FEET (1.5 M)

Depending on the species there are different measures and sizes. They measure around 3.3 to 5 feet (1 to 1.5 m) and weigh between 4.5 and 9 pounds (2 and 4 kg)

12 FEATHERS

Hidden under their wings are 12 black feathers which they use to fly.

A flamingo's plumage is nourished with a natural oil generated by a gland found at the base of the tail.

LEGS →

3 of the toes are joined to the others by a membrane. The 4th isn't, as it is used to maintain its balance.

Taxonomy

Phylum: **vertebrate**
Class: **bird**
Order: **phoenicopterifromes**

The legs are extremely thin and very long, and they grip the ground with four toes.

FLAMINGO
Sleeps on one leg

It is very social, living in colonies that may have populations of thousands of flamingos.

REPRODUCTION

It reproduces in areas where it is not disturbed and predators cannot reach the colony.

↓

They look for a new mate during each reproductive period. The male attracts a mate by waving its wings in greeting, showing off its colored parts.

↓

1 FOOT (30 CM)

They build nests up to 1 foot (30 cm) in height, using mounds of straw, feathers, and stones. It is cone-shaped, with a narrow base and a space in the center to house the egg.

↓

After six weeks the female lays a single egg, which takes between 27 and 31 days to incubate.

↓

The chicks are born with white down; as they grow, the plumage turns gray. In the adult stage it acquires its pinkish color.

Hours of sleep: intervals of minutes
Time of sleep: day and night

IT SLEEPS IN THE WATER AND ENTERS INTO A STATE OF REST.

It curls its neck and puts its beak under its wing, leaving one eye open to remain alert.

Its sleep is uni-hemispheric: one side of the brain rests and the other stays in a state of alert.

↓

It keeps its weight on one stiff leg. This posture helps it to regulate its body temperature. Every now and again, it unconsciously shifts its weight from one leg to another, to avoid muscular fatigue.

↓

It is able to quickly activate its joints and get out of that position if it needs to escape from a predator.

↓

While sleeping it maintains perfect balance: its body sways very little and its center of gravity shifts only a fraction of an inch.

GEOGRAPHICAL DISTRIBUTION

Found in America, Africa, Asia and Europe.

HABITAT

Lakes, coastal lagoons, estuaries, mangroves, sandy islands, and tidal plains.

It feeds on algae, crustaceans, insects, small fish, molluscs and plankton.

Most of these foods contain carotenoids.

A natural pigment that gives flamingos their characteristic pink plumage.

Scientific name: *Phoenicopterus*

Dietary type: **omnivore**

Life environment: **air**

Conservation status: **out of danger**

CROCODILE
SLEEPS WITH ONE EYE OPEN.

They are excellent swimmers. They usually live in slow-moving waters where they feed on a wide variety of animals.

Taxonomy

Phylum: **vertebrate**
Class: **reptile**
Order: **crocodilia**

THEY ARE POIKILOTHERMIC AND ECTOTHERMIC

In other words, their body temperature varies with their environment. The crocodiles' blood vessels are near the surface of their skin and they can regulate their temperature by keeping their mouths open.

3,968 POUNDS (1,800 KG) OF STRENGTH

New teeth grow to replace those that are broken or lost. Their bite is the most powerful in the whole animal kingdom.
They cannot chew, so they shake and tear their prey to pieces with their teeth.

Their eyes and nostrils are in the upper part of the head, which allows them to see and breathe while they are in the water. They can breathe while submerged, closing their nostrils, their inner ears, and a fold in their throat to prevent water from entering the lungs.

Its heart is formed of 4 cavities (two auricular and two ventricular).

They feed mainly on vertebrates (fish, reptiles and mammals) and sometimes invertebrates (molluscs and crustaceans).

REPRODUCTION

Fecundation is internal (meaning an embryo is formed inside the female): they are oviparous (meaning they lay eggs). They build nests from sticks and branches to hold the eggs.

Crocodiles appeared for the first time during the **Eoceno**, about 55 million years ago.

55
million
years

Scientific name: *Crocodylidae*	Type: **carnivore**	Life environment: **land, water**	Conservation status: **endangered**

Crocodiles lead quite inactive lives, remaining motionless most of the day. In the cool morning, crocodiles often bask in the heat of the sun on the riverbank.

Hours of sleep: 17 hours
Time of sleep: day

They like to sleep in shallow water. They keep their heads at the level of the water.

UNIHEMISPHERIC SLEEP

So-called because one side of the brain remains "awake", while the other half enters into a state of sleep.

It sleeps with one eye open, alert to threats in its surroundings.

It closes both eyes if it feels there is no danger nearby.

LIFE EXPECTANCY

50-80 YEARS

Its skin is hard, dry and scaly.

GEOGRAPHICAL DISTRIBUTION

Of all lung-breathing animals, it can spend the most time underwater. Its lungs are so large that it can stay submerged for up to 6 hours while moving continuously. Keeping still, it is capable of remaining 2 days underwater.

6h O+   2d O-

HABITAT

It lives in estuaries, rivers, deltas and lagoons.

Tropical areas of Africa, Asia, America and Australia.

They tend to congregate in freshwater habitats like rivers, lakes, wetlands and sometimes in salty water.

It is the only flying mammal. Unlike birds, it does not have hollow bones.

Fossil remains have been found dating back more than 52 million years.

52 million years

THEY ARE VERY IMPORTANT IN THE POLLINATION PROCESS. SINCE THEY DISTRIBUTE THE SEEDS OF MANY SPECIES OF PLANTS.

Bats' wings are thin and elastic, covering the whole body. The skin has muscular fibers, blood vessels, and nerves.

It has huge ears, 5 times larger than the size of its head.

It sees everything in black, white and shades of gray.

A lot of blood circulates through its wings: it is from there that bats take the energy and nutrients they need to fly.

The body is covered in very short fur that gives it protection against damp and cold.

The muscles inside their ears contract to stop their loud squeals from deafening them; and relax so they can hear the echoes they produce.

LIFE EXPECTANCY

UP TO 30 YEARS

UP TO 2.6 POUNDS (1.2 KG).

UP TO 5 FEET (1.5 M)

Bat excrement, known as guano, is one of the richest fertilizers.

THEY CAN FLY AT SPEEDS OF UP TO 30 MILES (50 KM) PER HOUR.

Taxonomy

Phylum: **vertebrate**
Class: **mammal**
Order: **chiroptera**

HABITAT

It lives in temperate and tropical climates. Forests, deserts, savannahs, prairies, pastures, urban and suburban areas.

IT LIVES IN COLONIES.

BAT
Sleeps hanging upside down

More than 1,100 species have been identified, on every continent.

Hours of sleep: 20 hours
Time of sleep: day

They sleep with their eyes closed, hanging upside down in the dark.

↓

Sleeping upside down is a survival mechanism; if they slept upright, they wouldn't be able to close their wings, or extend them to take flight.

↓

The tendons of their heels are joined to the rest of their body and easily grip surfaces, allowing them to stay in place with minimal effort.

↓

Blood does not rush to their heads, thanks to the veined valves of their circulatory system, which prevents gravity from causing it to pool.

↓

They can hibernate up to 183 days.
They usually sleep wrapped in their wings.

WHILE RESTING, THEIR VITAL FUNCTIONS DIMINISH NOTABLY.

Their hearts beat only 10 times per minute, in comparison with the 600 beats they reach while searching for food.

REPRODUCTION

Most bats have one pup a year, making them vulnerable to extinction. The female can find her pups among thousands of other bats because of their unique sound and smell.

The female hangs when it gives birth and catches her pup with its wings when it comes out.

Pups are born without fur and with its eyes closed.

30% FRUGIVORES

70% INSECTIVORES

They are able to catch between 500 and 1,000 insects an hour. Often, they eat a total number of insects equivalent to their body weight, helping to control the population of insects.

Depending on the species, they feed on fruit, insects, nectar, amphibians, birds and small mammals.

GEOGRAPHICAL DISTRIBUTION

Found on all continents apart from the Arctic, Antarctic and some isolated oceanic islands.

Scientific name: *Chiroptera*

Dietary type: **omnivore/carnivore**

Life environment: **air**

Conservation status: **vulnerable**

20 YEARS

UP TO 1.7 POUNDS (800 G).

Its weight is generally about 1.7 pounds (800 g).

UP TO 25 INCHES (63 CM)

Tip to tail, they usually measure 25 inches (63 cm), of which the beak is about 8 inches (20 cm).

8 INCHES (20 CM)

Its beak is long and reaches its full size after several months.

HABITAT

Humid and temperate woods in mountain ranges and low altitude tropical forests.

IT HAS A HUGE YELLOW BEAK WITH A BLACK SPOT. THE BEAK IS INCREDIBLY LIGHT. BECAUSE IT IS PRACTICALLY EMPTY INSIDE.

Its beak has little saw-like teeth, and its tongue is very long, measuring up to 5.5 inches (14 cm).

PROTECTED SPECIES IN THE NORTHEASTERN REGION OF ARGENTINA.

GEOGRAPHICAL DISTRIBUTION

It is found in the humid forests of east South America: northeastern Venezuela, the Guyanas, Bolivia, Paraguay, Brazil, northeastern Argentina, and Uruguay.

Its beak is made up of small hexagonal plates of a substance called keratin, which forms a structure similar to that of a sponge.

REPRODUCTION
- Oviparous reproduction.
- 2 to 4 eggs.
- The eggs hatch at between 16 and 20 days.
- The young are born naked and blind.
- Their growth is slow.
- The beak takes several months to develop.
- They open their eyes at 3 weeks.

Their cycle of reproduction is annual. To nest, they look for cavities in the trees which they usually use year after year. They are monogamous animals and live in couples.

The toucan is not a migratory bird: it is a sedentary species that lives in one single area all its life.

There is no sexual dimorphism between males and females: meaning they are undistinguishable from each other.

Taxonomy
Phylum: **vertebrate**
Class: **aves**
Order: **piciformes**

There are 6 genera and 42 different species of toucan.

TOUCAN

Thermal sleep

To sleep, it puts its beak on its shoulder and bends its tail. Other members of the flock are usually in nearby trees, so they can sleep like a family.

It has striking plumage, with a black body, a white throat and round blue eyes.

Its wings are small, short and round.

LEGS

It has 2 toes in front and 2 behind, making it easier to hold onto branches.

The tail is square in shape and moves easily up and down.

TAIL

It feeds mainly on fruit, but occasionally also eats insects, reptiles and the eggs of other birds.

It likes to sleep in tree hollows, looking for spots that keep it safe; hidden amongst the leaves and branches.

The eyes are surrounded by bright-colored skin. Sight is its most highly developed sense.

It closes its eyes for a few minutes, keeping alert to any unusual sound or movement.

While sleeping, its huge beak regulates its body temperature. When it is hot, blood accumulates in the blood vessels of the beak to make the bird cooler, and vice versa when it is cold.

Hours of sleep: intervals of minutes
Time of sleep: day

Scientific name: *Ramphastos Toco*

Dietary type: **omnivore**

Life environment: **air**

Conservation status: **out of danger**

29

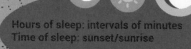

Hours of sleep: intervals of minutes
Time of sleep: sunset/sunrise

It rests in intervals of minutes, by unihemispheric sleep: where one part of the brain rests and the other part remains alert.

During sleep, its wingbeat is reduced from 10 movements per second to 7.

A HEIGHT OF 6,500 FEET (2,000 M)

It sleeps as it flies above the clouds. It reaches 6,500 feet (2,000 m) and slows the rhythm of its wings, letting itself fall in a spiral in a hovering state.

They are migratory birds, spending the summer in Europe, North Africa and Central Asia and the winter in southern Africa.

GEOGRAPHICAL DISTRIBUTION

Found in Europe, Asia and Africa.

It flies with its beak open, catching insects in its ample beak. Flies, fleas, spiders, caterpillars, beetles, moths and seeds are all food to this bird.

They mate in the air, repositioning the feathers of their wings and tail.

They lay 2 to 3 eggs and incubation lasts 18 to 20 days. The chicks, fed by their parents, fly after 35 days.

To feed its chicks, swifts mash its prey (some 300 insects) into a little ball behind the tongue. If food isn't available in its environment, a parent will fly for miles to look for food. While waiting, the chicks enter into a state of hibernation thanks to their reserves of fat.

Young swifts usually remain single from 2 to 4 years until they find a place to prepare their first nest.

THE COUPLES ARE MONOGAMOUS.

99%

HABITAT

Urban areas, cliffs, savannahs, prairies and near sources of water.

EXTREME MIGRANT

Its name comes from the fact that it spends 99% of its time in the air. It spends 10 months flying, and 3 months breeding.

UP TO
6.3
INCHES (16 CM)

Scientific name: **Apus Apus**

Dietary type: **omnivore**

Life environment: **air**

Conservation status: **out of danger**

BUILDS ITS NEST AT HEIGHT AND CAN MAINTAIN IT FOR MORE THAN 10 YEARS.

Because of their particular wing morphology and short legs, if swifts fall to the ground they experience great difficulty in getting back into flight, and need to do so from a high place.

Taxonomy

Phylum: **vertebrate**
Class: **aves**
Order: **apodiformes**

LIFE EXPECTANCY

The life expectancy of a swift is 11 years, although there are swifts who have lived to 21.

Its plumage is beautiful, with a small white or gray area under the beak.

It has long narrow wings in the shape of a half-moon.

Its tail is short, forked and deep..

AERODYNAMIC BODY

← TAIL

UP TO 21 YEARS

EYES

It has a very wide and large mouth with a small beak.

UP TO 62 MILES (100 KM) PER HOUR

It can reach sustained speeds of 62 miles (100 km) per hour. Its flight is unpredictable, with constant changes of direction.

BREAST AREA

UP TO 1.4 OUNCES (40 G)

It can weigh between 1.05 and 1.4 ounces (30 to 40 g)

Its feet have 4 toes pointing forward, equipped with powerful claws that it uses to grab things.

SWIFT
SLEEPS AS IT HOVERS

It flies and lives in a community, but hunts alone. Colonies can have up to 30 nests.

SLOTH

THE LONGEST SLEEPER

The 3-fingered sloth is a mammal, of which 4 species have been identified.

When it wakes up, it devotes itself to eating and looking for another branch where it can continue sleeping.

HABITAT

Misty, tropical lowland forests in the Amazon.

IT ONLY MOVES IN SEARCH OF SAFETY AND FOOD.

GEOGRAPHICAL DISTRIBUTION

Central and South America.

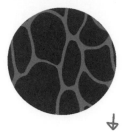

Taxonomy

Phylum: **vertebrate**
Class: **mammal**
Order: **pilosa**

270°

It is able to turn its head up to 270 degrees thanks to an additional vertebra in its neck.

The green coloration of the sloth are actually algae from the trees with which it forms a beneficial relationship. The algae find protection and water in the sloth's fur and they help camouflage it, protecting the sloth from predators.

Algae are not the only opportunists that settle on sloths: recent investigations have discovered that various fungi adhere to the sloth's fur too—some of which have curative properties.

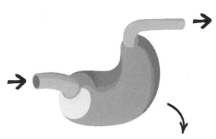

ITS STOMACH HAS FOUR PARTS AND HIGHLY SPECIALIZED INTESTINAL BACTERIA

They emit low sounds when they are trying to protect their habitat or are in search of a mate.

They eat very slowly and copiously due to the lack of nutritional value of their food. They need water to drink, and mostly obtain it from the vegetation they consume.

THEY CAN WEIGH UP TO **11** POUNDS (5 KG)

REPRODUCTION

They only mix during mating or while the female is looking after her pups. They mate while hanging from the tree. 6 months later, the pup is born and becomes independent at 9 months.

LIFE EXPECTANCY

30 YEARS

They can live up to 30 years in captivity, and up to 15 in the wild.

It only comes down to the ground 2 or 3 times a week. It swims very well and moves more quickly in water than in trees or on the ground.

Its front paws help it to defend itself in case a fight breaks out.

It likes the top part of the trees, looking for branches with lots of leaves in order to pass unnoticed.

Hours of sleep: 20 hours
Time of sleep: night

In its sleep, a growth hormone is released.

6.5 FEET (2 M) PER MINUTE

On the ground, it moves at 6.5 feet (2 m) per minute and in the trees 10 feet (3 m) per minute.

Thanks to the claws on its feet, it can hang from the most unlikely shapes.

It usually sleeps with other sloths, each hanging from a different branch.

It has claws on 3 toes. They are very sharp, designed for climbing and hanging.

IT IS COMMON TO SEE THE SLOTH HANGING UPSIDE DOWN FROM THE BRANCHES OF TREES.

2.6
FEET (80 CM)

It eats the produce of trees, like fruit and a variety of leaves.

Scientific name: *Bradypus Variegatus*

Dietary type: **herbivore**

Life environment: **land**

Conservation status: **endangered**

Taxonomy

Phylum: **vertebrate**
Class: **mammal**
Order: **primate**

The shape of the body is characterized by its sturdiness. The stomach area is larger than its chest and its head is wider at the top, due to a very pronounced sagittal crest (a bone in its forehead).

THEY LIKE FLAT TERRAIN, WHERE THEY CAN MOVE MORE EASILY. THEY ONLY CLIMB TO REACH A SOURCE OF FOOD.

The fur is dark in color, black, brown, or gray. It is shorter around the nose and lips, as well as on the chest, the ears, the palms of the feet, the hands, and the fingers.

UP TO
440
POUNDS
(200 KG).

They weigh between 310 and 440 pounds (140 to 200 kg). The female weighs approximately half what the male weighs.

They have small ears and a nose with wrinkles around it that are unique to each individual.

A gorilla's arms are longer than its legs. They walk on their knuckles, putting all their weight through their arms.

THEY HAVE FIVE FINGERS ON EACH HAND AND FIVE TOES ON EACH FOOT.

Like humans, they have unique fingerprints and nails instead of claws.

UP TO
8.7
FEET (1.75 M)

They can stand up on two legs and every now and then walk or run a short distance in a vertical position.

They measure between 5.4 AND 8.7 feet (1.65 and 1.75 m).

Recent studies have shown that gorillas and humans are about 98% similar their DNA.

GORILLA

CHANGES ITS DEN WITH EVERY SLEEP.

Hours of sleep: 8 hours
Time of sleep: night

It sleeps at night, with its eyes closed and in the same way as humans: on its side, stretched out, or face up with one hand behind the head, among other positions.

LIVES IN A TROOP

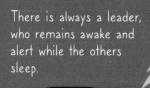

They live in troops with an average of 10 members, with one or two adult males, various adult females, and their young. There is a strong and permanent relationship between the members of the group. They communicate with a variety of verbal and non-verbal methods.

Fossils show that gorillas appeared for the first time in Africa more than 12 million years ago.

12 MILLION YEARS

EVERY NIGHT THE FEMALE SPENDS 10 MINUTES PREPARING THE BED:

Before sleeping she prepares the place she will use as a den, with leaves and tree branches. They never sleep twice in the same place.

The dominant male chooses where he will sleep and then the others take their places around him.

There is always a leader, who remains awake and alert while the others sleep.

The leader of the troop assumes responsibility for fighting in order to protect them, and will do so with his life if necessary.

SILVERBACK GORILLA

It is a species of mature male, no younger than 15 years. It is very well known for its short white and silver fur.

THERE ARE ONLY TWO REMAINING SPECIES OF SILVERBACK GORILLAS IN THE WORLD.

LIFE EXPECTANCY

UP TO 30 YEARS

REPRODUCTION

A newborn baby weighs between 3.3 and 6.6 pounds (1.5 and 3 kg). It is looked after until it is 2 or 3. On average, a female gives birth to one gorilla every 4 years.

GESTATION PERIOD 8.5 MONTHS

HABITAT

Gorillas live in tropical and subtropical forests, in lowlands, marshes and mountains.

GEOGRAPHICAL DISTRIBUTION

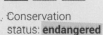

Found in east and west Africa

They feed on leaves, roots, grasses, trees and fruit.

Scientific name: **Gorilla**

Dietary type: **herbivore**

Life environment: **land**

Conservation status: **endangered**

THEY DRINK LITTLE WATER

They can spend up to three days without doing so, since they obtain it from their food.

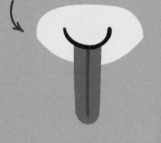

They reach a height of between 13 and 20 feet (4 and 6 m).

UP TO 20 FEET (6 M)

They have tongues that measure between 20 and 20.8 inches (50 and 53 cm). The color varies between shades of black, brown, and blue. They are impervious to the thorns contained in the leaves and branches with which they feed themselves.

HABITAT

It lives in pastures, savannahs, prairies, forests and warm plains.

LIFE EXPECTANCY

UP TO 30 YEARS

Its life expectancy is between 25 and 30 years.

Taxonomy

Phylum: **vertebrate**
Class: **mammal**
Order: **artiodactyla**

← HORNS

It has two horns on its head which serve to distinguish the sex.

The females have the top of their horns covered with hair. The males do not, due to the fact that they lose their hair in fights for females.

VERTEBRAE

They have very long, flexible necks, due to their seven vertebrae, which usually measure 11 inches (28 cm) each.

They have 4 stomachs and a digestive process that is very slow, with various stages. First they chew the food and swallow it to process it, then they pass the chewed food back up into the neck and chew it again in the mouth.

Giraffe's coats are smooth and yellow or brown in color, with darker spots that vary between species and between animals.

No two giraffes look the same: they each have a different pattern of spots on their body.

THEY CAN WEIGH UP TO 4,188 POUNDS (1,900 KG).

The males weigh about 4,188 pounds (1,900 kg), and the females about 2,545 pounds (1,200 kg).

← LEGS

ITS LEGS MEASURE 6.5 FEET (2 M).

Their strong muscles and sharp hooves are effective weapons of defense.

UP TO 39 INCHES (100 CM)

Its tail measures from 30 to 39 inches (78 to 100 cm).

← HOOVES

GIRAFFE

Sleeps standing up to survive

There are 4 distinct species: southern giraffe, Masai giraffe, reticulated giraffe and northern giraffe.

THEY HAVE A LOCKING MECHANISM IN THEIR JOINTS WHICH ALLOWS THEM TO MINIMIZE EFFORT IN THE MUSCLES WHEN THEY SLEEP STANDING UP.

Hours of sleep: 2 to 4 hours
Time of sleep: nigh

They sleep at night in naps of 5 to 10 minutes.

They usually sleep standing up, due to their large size and the length of their necks.

They rest with one eye open, alert for predators.

They live in herds of 10 members. These groups consist of females and 1 or 2 young males. After a year, the young can change herd constantly, without there being any difficulties in mutual recognition.

THEY CAN GO FOR WEEKS WITHOUT SLEEPING

On rare occasions they lie down to sleep, but not completely, since that would it make it hard for them to escape a predator.

When they do this, they bend their legs and rest their heads on the lower part of the body.

REPRODUCTION

The gestation period of giraffes is 15 months and they have a single calf. The female gives birth to her young standing up and the calf falls to the ground from about 8 feet (2.5 m).

15 MONTHS GESTATION

JUST ONE CALF

It can ingest 66 pounds (30 kg) at a time, and can eat more than 132 pounds (60 kg) daily.

The males fight for territory and for the order of mating, hitting each other with their long necks.

They feed on leaves and fresh fruit from trees. Their main nutrition consists of myrrh and acacia.

GEOGRAPHICAL DISTRIBUTION

Found on the African continent.

Scientific name: *Giraffa Camelopardia*

Dietary type: **herbivore**

Life environment: **land**

Conservation status: **vulnerable**

UP TO 70 YEARS

LIFE EXPECTANCY

THEY FORM GROUPS WITH VERY STRONG EMOTIONAL TIES, IN WHICH THEY LOOK AFTER EACH OTHER, TRAVEL AND INTERACT.

HABITAT

They live in all the oceans of the world, in deep areas, deep-sea pits, and underwater canyons in tropical, temperate, and cold waters.

UP TO 65 FEET (20 M)

UP TO 50 TONS

The males measure between 52 and 65 feet (16 and 20 m) and weigh up to 50 tons. The females measure from 36 to 46 feet (11 to 14 m) and weigh on average 25 tons.

GEOGRAPHICAL DISTRIBUTION

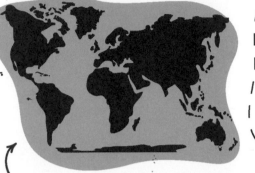

Found in the Pacific, Atlantic, Indian and Antarctic Oceans.

REPRODUCTION

The gestation period lasts 15 months. They give birth to a single calf.

The lactation period extends up to 2 years.

The females are very protective of their calves and work together to ensure their care. One or two females dive down to bring food up to the youngest, while the others look after the calves.

Giving birth is a social event in which the rest of the group forms a protective barrier around the mother and the newborn calf.

They are extremely large, their heads are square in outline.

BLOWHOLE

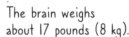

The brain weighs about 17 pounds (8 kg).

It can easily dive vertically to about 4,920 feet (1,500 m).

7-7.8 INCHES (18 TO 20 CM)

The teeth in the lower jaw are between 7 and 7.8 inches (18 and 20 cm) long. There are no teeth in the upper jaw.

They feed on squid, fish, octopus, and eels. They can consume up to 2,205 pounds (1,000 kg) of food a day.

THE BODY IS ROUGH AND MAY HAVE SCARRING. THEY HAVE WIDE SHORT PECTORAL FINS AND A LARGE CAUDAL FIN.

Scientific name: **Physeter Macrocephalus**

Dietary type: **carnivore**

Life environment: **water**

Conservation status: **endangered**

The pulmonary system is not connected to the mouth. This allows them to feed without water getting into their lungs.

↓

When whales sleep they close their blowholes, so that no water gets into their lungs.

They come up to the surface to breathe through the blowhole.

Hours of sleep: naps of 10 to 12 minutes
Time of sleep: day and night

THEY SLEEP IN A VERTICAL POSITION, IN A SEMI-RESTING STATE

When they sleep, only one of their hemispheres enters into a state of rest.

↓

They keep one eye open. This helps them both to keep sight of their surroundings and to protect themselves against predators.

↓

They float near the surface when they sleep, in groups of 5 or 6.

CAUDAL FIN

They swim at a speed of 3 to 9 miles (5 to 15 km) per hour. When they accelerate, they can reach 28 miles (45 km) per hour.

← ← ←

Their food dregs float to the surface and disperse, to be consumed by phytoplankton and fertilizing the ocean in the process.

They have a system of echo localization similar to a sonar, which is how they interpret what an object is.

Taxonomy

Phylum: **vertebrate**
Class: **mammal**
Order: **artiodactyla**

PECTORAL FIN

The males are the only ones that swim in the cold waters of the poles. The females and the young remain in tropical and temperate areas.

SPERM WHALE

SLEEPS IN A VERTICAL POSITION

Hours of sleep: 5/7 months during hibernation
Time of sleep: day and night

They sleep in rocky areas of forests, in caves, on the slopes of hills, in hollow trunks and cavities in the earth.

During the summer, they rest in the coolest parts of the forest.

They feed during the summer to accumulate fat and be able to hibernate in the winter.

Most of their activities are carried out at dusk or during the night, although they can also be active during the day.

HIBERNATION

During the winter they enter into a period of hibernation, reducing their metabolic rhythm by 53%.

Their pulse rate is reduced from 90 to 8 per minute.

In this period they do not drink, eat or even defecate, but they do remain alert to any situation, so that they can react to danger.

THEY HAVE STRONG BODIES AND SHORT LEGS. THEY WALK ON ALL FOURS.

Depending on the species, they have thick, abundant, rough fur: yellow, reddish, black, white and with spots.

They adapt to their habitat to regulate their body temperature and blend in with their surroundings.

UP TO 110 POUNDS (50 KG).

Their weight varies from 66 to 110 pounds (30 to 50 kg). The largest reach over 1,750 pounds (800 kg). The females weigh up to 20% less than the males.

UP TO 10 FEET (3 M)

If they rise up on their hind legs, they easily reach 6.5 to 10 feet (2 to 3 m).

UP TO 25 MILES PER HOUR (40 KM/H)

They can reach a speed of up to 25 miles (40 km) per hour.

They are solitary, calm, and curious. Only the females are accompanied by their cubs.

BEAR
SLEEPS IN ITS WINTER REFUGE

There are 8 species of bear: panda bear, spectacled bear, sun bear, sloth bear, Asiatic black bear, American black bear, brown bear and polar bear.

After hibernation, they move to a state of "mobile hibernation", as if they were dazed; they stay like this for several weeks until the body recovers.

Their heads are impressive, characterized by small round ears and long narrow snouts.

Taxonomy

Phylum: **vertebrate**
Class: **mammal**
Order: **carnivora**

REPRODUCTION

The females keep their cubs with them during hibernation, in mid-winter, and suckle them in the den until spring.

THEY CAN HAVE 2 TO 3 CUBS.

↓

Bears mate in the spring and after a brief period in which the embryo develops, the females experience so-called "delayed implantation", which slows the embryo's development by several months.

⇓

When the female has stored sufficient energy in the form of fat for herself and her cubs to survive the winter, only then does the embryo become a cub.

Its eyesight is not every well developed, but both its hearing and its sense of smell are very good.

It has fangs and fearsome jaws, adapted to a diet of meat and vegetables.

HABITAT - - - →

They live in tropical woods, mountains, prairies, scrubland, mountains and in the Arctic tundra.

LIFE EXPECTANCY

UP TO 30 YEARS

Their life expectancy is from 20 to 30 years.

GEOGRAPHICAL DISTRIBUTION

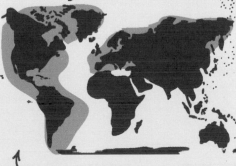

Found in North America, South America, Europe, Asia and the Arctic.

The panda bear feeds on bamboo, lizards and rodents.
The polar bear feeds on seals, wolves and roots.
The sloth bear feeds on ants and termites.
The other species feed on meat, fish, eggs, honey, insects and plants.

Scientific name: *ursidae*

Dietary type: **omnivore**

Life environment: **land**

Conservation status: **vulnerable**

UP TO 80 YEARS

LIFE EXPECTANCY

UP TO **13** FEET (4 M)

UP TO **13,000** POUNDS (6,000 KG).

They can measure up to 13 feet (4 m) and weigh between 11,000 and 13,000 pounds (5,000 and 6,000 kg).

HABITAT

They live in forests in tropical and subtropical climates, prairies, river valleys, pastures, and savannas.

GEOGRAPHICAL DISTRIBUTION

Found in Africa and Asia.

Elephants are highly intelligent. They exhibit behavior such as mourning the dead, forming relationships with other members of the herd, using tools and playing.

They move their ears to cool down. Their ears act as a thermostat, helping them to cope with the strong heat of the areas where they live.

Their first teeth fall out when they are 3 years old. At this point, their adult teeth emerge and keep growing, all their lives, at an average speed of 6 inches (15 cm) per year

. They have one of the best senses of smell in the animal kingdom, with 2,000 genes devoted to it.

The trunk is one of the most powerful anatomical structures in the animal kingdom. It has more than 100,000 muscles, it is used like a long arm with which they access water to drink — and to sprinkle on themselves when it is hot.

Taxonomy

Phylum: **vertebrate**
Class: **mammal**
Order: **proboscidea**

They are classified into two distinct genera, with one species identified in each of them: the African elephant and the Asian elephant.

ELEPHANT

Sleeps according to the climate.

RESTS WITH ITS HERD.

They regularly choose different places to rest in and one member always remains on the alert.

↓

A scientific study has discovered that they lie down to sleep every three or four days for one hour, this is the only time they reach REM sleep.

IT SLEEPS LYING DOWN OR STANDING UP VERY CLOSE TO A TREE IN ORDER TO SUPPORT ITSELF.

Their sleep is dependent on environmental factors like temperature, humidity and wind.

Hours of sleep: 2 hours
Time of sleep: night

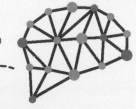

They usually sleep at night, mainly between 2 and 6 in the morning.

↓

If danger lurks they can go two days without sleep.

The REM (rapid eye movement) phase is a phase of sleep which is character-ized by the presence of increased cerebral activity that shows itself as a series of rapid and constant eye movements.

THEY LIVE IN HERDS OF SOME TWENTY MEMBERS.

They have very complex social lives. Herds are matriarchal, with females remaining together all their lives.

The groups are semi-permanent; they separate from time to time during journeys and then meet up again after a while.

It feeds with leaves of trees, soft crusts, fruits, herbs, stems, roots and all kinds of vegetables.

REPRODUCTION

Gestation lasts approximately 22 or 23 months and is the longest gestation of all mammals and land species.

↓

Inside the womb, the calf measures 3.5 feel (1 m) and weighs approximately 264 pounds (120 kg).

↓

At birth, they are very independent. They can survive by themselves right from the start.

↓

The females wait 4 or 5 years before becoming pregnant again: throughout their lives they can give birth to between 7 and 12 calves.

ELEPHANTS CAN REMEMBER

They have exceptional memories; they remember the voice and smell of other individuals of their species, human faces, and the routes they have previously taken in search of food.

Scientific name: *Elephantidae*

Dietary type: **herbivore**

Life environment: **land**

Conservation status: **vulnerable**

The females bond closely, bringing up their cubs together. These prides can have between 4 and 37 members.

The females go hunting in search of food for all the members of their group. The male lion is always the first to eat and what is left over will be devoured by the lionesses.

Their skeleton gives them agility thanks to a flexible spinal column. Their body is adapted to attack with more force than resistance. It has large muscles in its thighs that allow them to attack standing up.

REPRODUCTION

Mating between males and females lasts several days.

The gestation period lasts 3.5 months.

LIONESSES CAN HAVE A CUB EVERY 2 YEARS.

It usually has between 1 to 6 cubs.
At birth, they weigh between 42 and 70 ounces (1,200 and 2,000 g).

The mother moves her cub from place to place, to avoid leaving its smell in one area and attracting predators.

LIFE EXPECTANCY

UP TO **20** YEARS

UP TO **573** POUNDS (260 KG)

UP TO **10** FEET (3 M)

It weighs between 573 and 264 pounds (120 and 260 kg) and measures up to 10 feet (3 m) in length (head-body-tail)

THEY ARE THE MOST SOCIABLE OF FELINES

Prides are made up of females, cubs and lions with one leader. It is responsible for the safety of the group within its territory.

GEOGRAPHICAL DISTRIBUTION

Found in Africa, with some populations in Asia.

HABITAT

Lives in grassland, open forests, plains, scrubland and savannahs.

They can ingest up to 17 pounds (8 kg) of meat a day.

Taxonomy

Phylum: **vertebrate**
Class: **mammal**
Order: **carnivore**

There are 2 differentiated species: African lion and Asian lion.

LION
SLEEPS TO HUNT AGAIN.

44

THEY REST IN PLACES WITH TREES, BRANCHES, ROCKS AND SHORT UNDERGROWTH.

Of all the felines in the world, they have the most powerful roar.

Hours of sleep: 13 hours
Time of sleep: day and night

They tend to sleep more during the day, with the body stretched out and the eyes closed.

Their whiskers allow them to smell and to find their way in the dark.

The duration of their sleep depends on the time they spend on digestion.

They are nocturnal, they hunt after nightfall when the temperature goes down.

Their powerful jaws have sharp fangs 3 inches (8 cm) long.

They have a very good sense of hearing. They can turn their ears in various directions, picking up different sounds in their environment.

Their paws are broad and strong, with retractable claws adapted for capturing prey and puncturing the skin of their victims.

They have sinewy bodies with short, broad noses.

They feed on large animals like zebras, buffalo, impalas, gnus, rodents, reptiles, hyenas, leopards and occasionally giraffes.

Scientific name: *Panthera Leo*

Dietary type: **carnivore**

Life environment: **land**

Conservation status: **vulnerable**

They have good eyesight and excellent hearing. When a member of the mob is in danger, it warns the others by hitting the ground with its feet.

Name given to the large social groups in which they live.

A kangaroo uses its incisors to cut grass and chew it repeatedly to make it digestible. The stomach is very big and can accommodate large quantities of food. Kangaroos obtain water from vegetables and can go for long periods without drinking.

UP TO 43 MILES (70 KM) PER HOUR

Their speed is from 12 to 15 miles (20 to 25 km) per hour on long distances, but they can reach speeds of up to 43 miles (70 kmk) an hour at short distances.

Thanks to their body structure, kangaroos can only move forward – never backward.

They have two forelegs and two hind legs which they use for hopping and moving about, as well as a tail that allows them to keep their balance.

The males have strong backs and shoulders. Their forelegs are much smaller, although they are powerful and equipped with sharp claws.

The tibia bone of the kangaroo's hind legs is twice as long as the femur and forms a kind of Z shape. This bone has pads of fibrous cartilage which act as shock absorbers.

THEY CAN WEIGH UP TO **187** POUNDS (85 KG)

With each hop they cover a distance of approximately 6.5 feet (2 m). When they flee from a predator they can cover a distance of 29.5 feet (9 m).

0   2M   9M

HIND LEGS

6.5 FEET (2 M)

TAIL

The tail is muscular and can be as long as the whole body. They use it to control their hopping and to move at low speeds, as if it were another leg. It can easily support the whole weight of the body.

LIFE EXPECTANCY

UP TO **16** YEARS

Taxonomy

Phylum: **vertebrate**
Class: **mammal**
Order: **diprotodontia**

There are three species: the red kangaroo, the eastern gray kangaroo and the western gray kangaroo.

KANGAROO

TAKES NAPS IN THE GRASS.

Hours of sleep: naps of 5 to 10 minutes, over a period of 2 hours
Time of sleep: day

During periods of drought they regulate their blood chemistry to survive – they can even become infertile for entire seasons.

Looking for shelter from the sun, kangaroos sleep under trees or in the grass. Often, they dig shallow holes in which to have a nap and beat the heat.

They have various positions for resting: on their sides, lying down, with their front legs beneath their heads, on their backs, curled up.

REPRODUCTION

The female has a ventral pouch in her belly area, in which she accommodates her joey during the first months until it develops and reaches maturity.

PREGNANCY LASTS APPROXIMATELY 35 DAYS

The newborn kangaroo is called a "neonate" because it is not completely formed and cannot survive outside its mother's belly, but must immediately go into the mothers pouch.

The newborn is tiny, blind, without ears or hair; it does have a sense of smell though and strong front legs with claws which help it to get to the pouch on its mother's belly.

The pouch functions as an incubator where the joey will eat and live for the first six months of life. When it is ready, it will emerge from the pouch but continue to suckle.

A second baby kangaroo can be born in 24 hours after the firstborn has abandoned the pouch. Each one will suckle from a different teat with a different composition of milk appropriate to its growth stage.

A MALE CAN IMPREGNATE UP TO 20 FEMALES.

The male courts the female by fighting or boxing with other males for mating rights.

Young mother kangaroos gives birth to females, as they grow older they will give birth to males.

GEOGRAPHICAL DISTRIBUTION

Found in New Guinea, Tasmania and Australia.

It feeds during the night on grass, roots and many species of plants.

HABITAT
They live in dry zones like steppes and savannahs, although they are also found in dry forests and prairies.

Scientific name: *Macropodidae*

Dietary type: **herbivore**

Life environment: **land**

Conservation status: **out of danger**

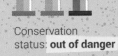

THEY ALL SLEEP

Sleep is the time when the senses and movements are suspended.

Sleep is a phase of extreme inactivity impacted by an animals' characteristics: size, shape, and neural states. Not all species require the same hours of sleep, since they do not have the same needs. So their rest time depends on various factors, like their food or their distinct ways of life. The rhythm of their sleep is also affected by body temperature and heart rate.

In mammals there are three states of sleep: wakefulness, slow sleep, and para-doxical sleep (REM or dream state).

Carnivores sleep for longer since they run less risk of being attacked, unlike herbivores who have to remain alert for predators.

Large animals sleep much less due to the fact that they need to spend time eating more. Many species have the ability to sleep by resting just one hemisphere of their brain, keeping the other one active.

Other species . . .

Fruit fly/10h

Pigeon/11h

Cheetah/12h

Cat/12h

Duck-billed platypus/14h

Dolphin/10h

Dog/10h

Parrotfish/8h

Sheep/4h

Cow/5h

Whether on land, water or air, each species has its own way of sleeping.

Koala / 22h

Armadillo / 19h

Opossum / 19h

Hedgehog / 18h

Squirrel / 15h

Shrew / 16h

Lemur / 16h

Tiger / 16h

Rat / 14h

Owl / 13h

Rabbit / 11h

Duck / 11h

Chimpanzee / 8h

Pig / 8h

Seal / 6h

Zebra / 3h

Goat / 5h

Horse / 3h

Hours

24
23
22
21
20
19
18
17
16
15
14
13
12
11
10
9
8
7
6
5
4
3
2
1
0

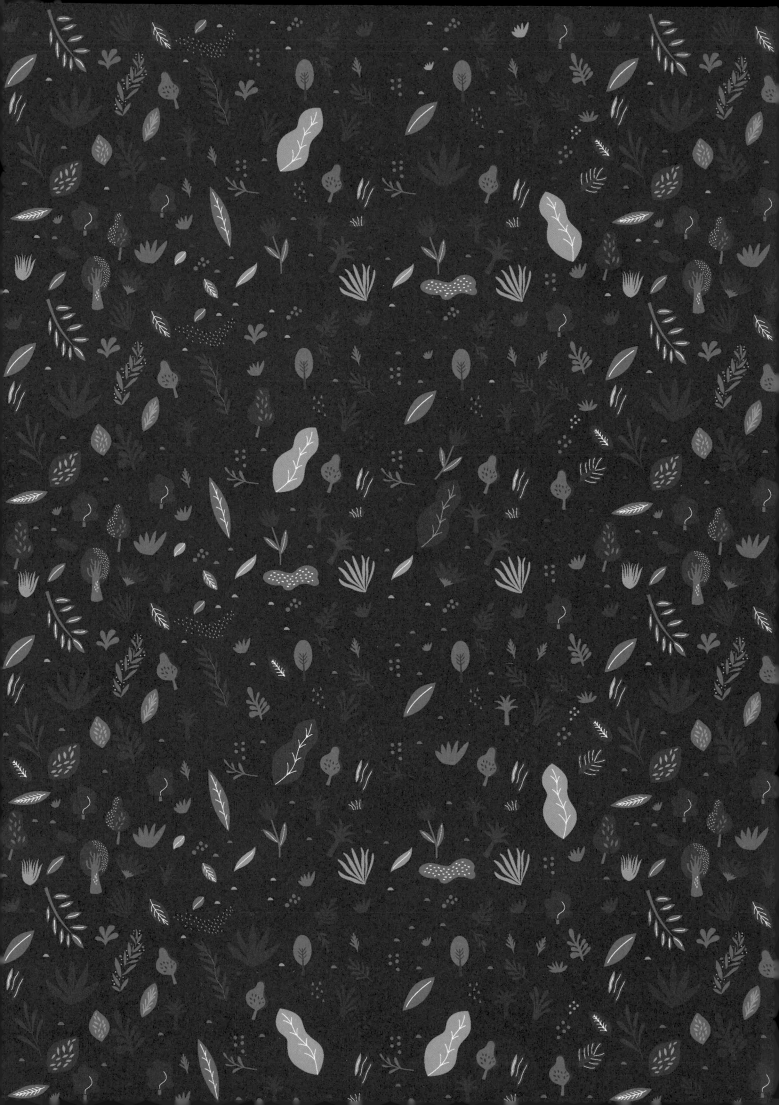